Felix Mendelssohn–Bartholdy
(1809–1847)

Songs without Words

Romances sans paroles
Lieder ohne Worte

I

for piano • pour piano • für Klavier

K 127

6 Lieder ohne Worte, Op. 19B

1. Andante con moto — 4
2. Andante espressivo — 9
3. Molto allegro e vivace — 12
4.  Moderato — 16
5. Piano agitato — 18
6. Venetianisches Gondellied — Andante sostenuto — 24

6 Lieder ohne Worte, Op. 30

1. Andante espressivo — 26
2. Allegro di molto — 28
3. Adagio non troppo — 31
4. Agitato e con fuoco — 32

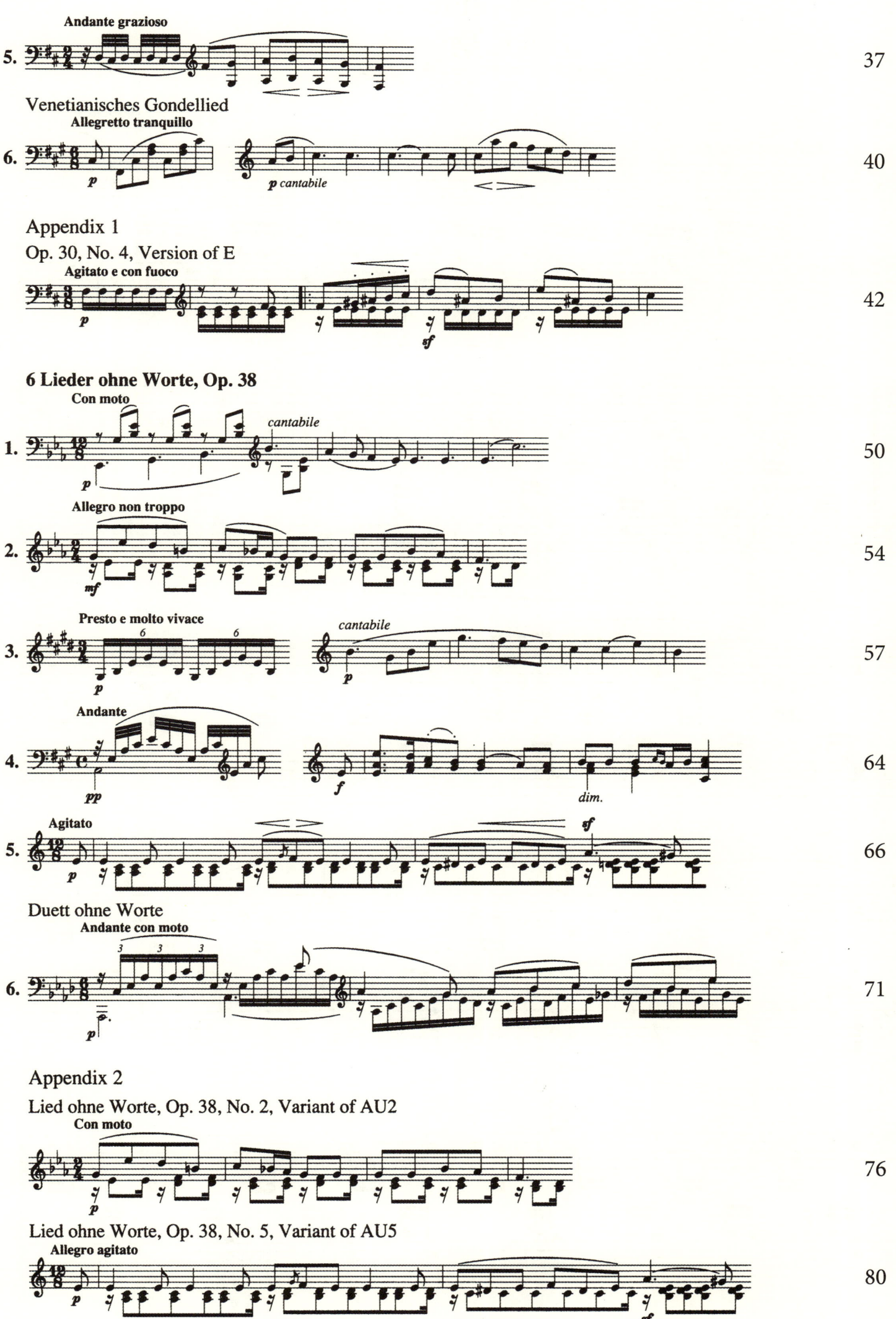

6 Lieder ohne Worte
[Heft I], Op. 19B
First Publication: London, 1832

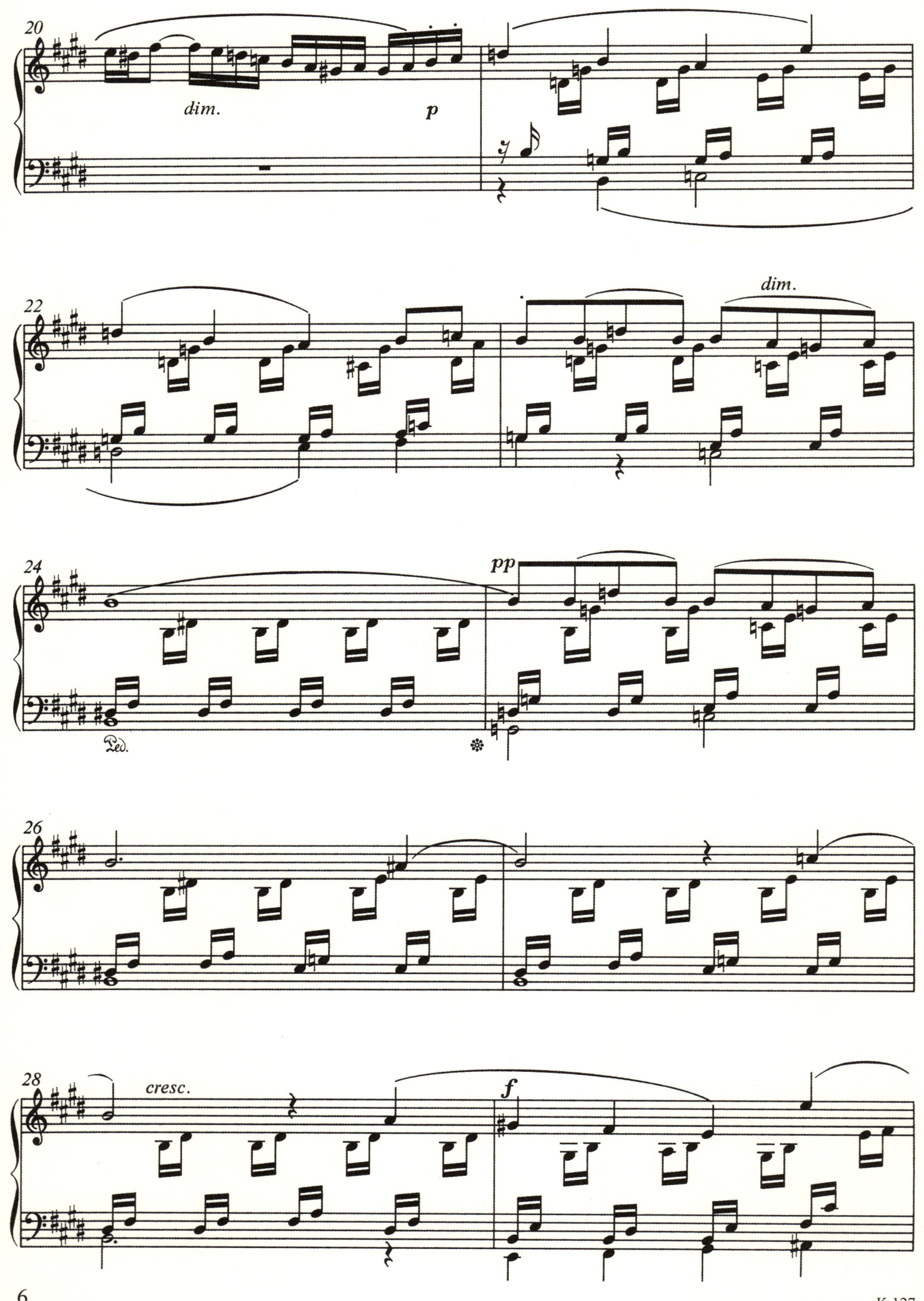

Op. 19B, No. 4

Op. 19B, No. 5

K 127

19

Venetianisches Gondellied
In a Gondola – Barcarolle

Op. 19B, No. 6

Elise von Woringen zugeeignet

6 Lieder ohne Worte
Heft II, Op. 30
First publication: Bonn, 1835

Op. 30, No. 1

Venetianisches Gondellied
Barcarolle

Op. 30, No. 6

Lied ohne Worte, Op. 30, No. 4. Version of AU4.
SBPK, Mus. ms. autogr. F. Mendelssohn Bartholdy 28, pp. 151–152.

Appendix 1

Op. 30, No. 4
Version of E

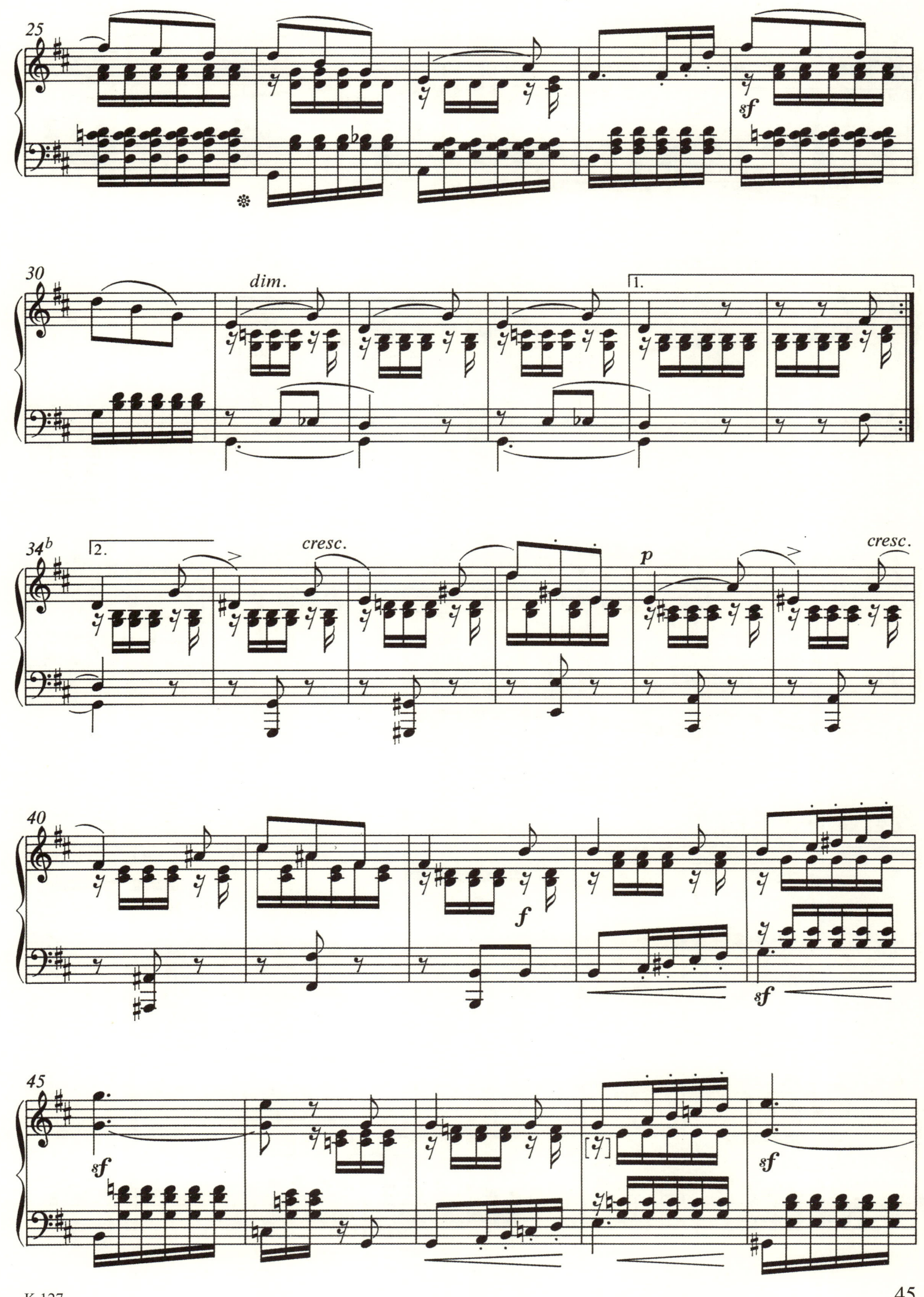

Rosa von Woringen zugeeignet

6 Lieder ohne Worte
Heft III, Op. 38
First publication: Bonn, 1837

Op. 38, No. 3

Duett ohne Worte

Op. 38, No. 6

Appendix 2

An Henriette Grabau

Lied ohne Worte

Op. 38, No. 2
Variant of AU2
29.Mar.1836, Frühfassung

Lied ohne Worte, Op. 38, No. 5. Version of AU5.
SBPK, Mus. ms. autogr. F. Mendelssohn Bartholdy 29, p. 135.

Lied ohne Worte

Op. 38, No. 5
Variant of AU5
05. Apr. 1837, Frühfassung

**OVER 25.000 PAGES OF PIANO
MUSIC SHEETS ONLINE**

Bach, Beethoven, Brahms, Chopin, Czerny,
Debussy, Gershwin, Dvořák, Grieg, Haydn,
Joplin, Lyadov, Mendelssohn-Bartholdy, Mozart,
Mussorgsky, Purcell, Schubert, Schumann,
Scriabin, Tchaikovsky and many more

KÖNEMANN

© 2018 koenemann.com GmbH
www.koenemann.com

Editor: István Máriássy
Responsible co-editor: Tamás Záskaliczky
Technical editor: Dezső Varga
Engraved by Kottamester Bt., Budapest

ISBN 978-3-7419-1483-6

Printed in China by Reliance Printing

K 127